JUNETEENTH

Grandfather and grandson enjoy Juneteenth, Galveston, 1995.

JUNETEENTH

Freedom Day

Muriel Miller Branch

Photographs by Willis Branch

COBBLEHILL/Dutton

New York

Photograph Credits

Austin History Center, 12, 17, 22, 23, 25; Muriel Miller Branch, 36;
Reproduced from the Collections of the Library of Congress, 5 (top), 8,
14, 32, 34; Rosenberg Library, 2, 5 (bottom), 20, 33. All other photographs by Willis Branch.

Library of Congress Cataloging-in-Publication Data

Branch, Muriel Miller.
    Juneteenth: freedom day / Muriel Miller Branch ;
photographs by Willis Branch.
        p.   cm.
    Includes bibliographical references and index.
    Summary: Discusses the origin and present-day celebration of
Juneteenth, a holiday marking the day Texan slaves realized they were free.
    ISBN 0-525-65222-1
    1. Juneteenth—Juvenile literature. 2. Slaves—Emancipation—Texas—
Galveston—Juvenile literature. 3. Afro-Americans—History—Juvenile literature. 4. Afro-Americans—Social life and customs—Juvenile literature. [1. Juneteenth. 2. Afro-Americans—Social life and customs. 3. Slavery—Texas. 4.
Texas—Social life and customs.]   I. Title.
E185.93.T4B68   1998
394.263—dc21   97-9656
                                                              CIP
                                                              AC

Published in the Unted States by Cobblehill Books,
an affiliate of Dutton Children's Books,
a member of Penguin Putnam Inc.,
375 Hudson Street, New York, New York 10014

Designed by Joy Taylor

Printed in Hong Kong
First edition   10   9   8   7   6   5   4   3   2   1

To my husband, Willis

To my daughter Sonja

To my two beautiful granddaughters,

Nikki and Erica

To my mother, Missouri

To my brothers, Frank and Arthur

To my kin — immediate and distant,

I thrive on your collective love.

Acknowledgments

I THANK all of the persons in Texas, Arizona, Virginia, Maryland, Washington, D.C., California, and South Carolina, who shared their Juneteenth stories and experiences. I am especially grateful to the kind people of Galveston, Texas, including the Williams family and the staff at the Rosenberg Library. I deeply appreciate the assistance of the personnel at the Library of Congress, the State Library of Virginia, and Virginia Commonwealth University. I thank Eva Mae Ashabranner for making me aware of Juneteenth in Arizona, and Willie Barner of Los Angeles, California, for his vivid recollection of the Juneteenths of his childhood. I am also indebted to my friend and co-worker Earlene G. Evans for reading those rough drafts, and for allowing me to bounce ideas off of her. I am perhaps most indebted to Representative Al Edwards for carrying out his vision of making Juneteenth a legal holiday in Texas. Lastly, I thank all those Texans who have migrated to other parts of the country and have carried with them this wonderful celebration of freedom.

Contents

Juneteenth

A Juneteenth parade in Galveston, Texas. Race pride—unidentified girls in African attire.

CHAPTER

1
___

My husband, Willis, and I arrived in Houston, Texas, the day after the Houston Rockets won their second consecutive NBA championship. We had come to Texas to experience Juneteenth. But in a town gone wild with Rocket fever, we wondered if that was going to be possible. Rocket mania overshadowed everything! Juneteenth, the grandfather of all holidays for Black Texans, the one for which work has been halted and towns have shut down for more than 130 years, had been upstaged by the Rockets' stunning win over the Orlando Magic.

What if there wasn't going to be a Juneteenth? we worried. In desperation, we started asking anyone who would stop to talk to us if Juneteenth was still going to be celebrated.

"Where are the Juneteenth celebrations being held?" we asked a number of young people who worked in the hotel.

"Juneteenth? Well, I don't know," or "Haven't seen anything in the paper about it yet," they responded vaguely. They seemed to be totally out of touch with Juneteenth.

We repeated the same question so many times that we must have sounded like a record with the needle stuck in the same groove. Nobody could tell us about Juneteenth. So, maybe Juneteenth wasn't such a big deal in Texas after all, we thought.

We spent a miserable first night in Houston, afraid that perhaps we had made this trip in vain. The next morning our search for Juneteenth began again.

"Do you know where Juneteenth is being held?" we asked the elderly waiter who was serving us.

"We been havin' Juneteenth all month," he answered. "Matter of fact, there's a gospelfest in the park tomorrow night."

"Park?" we asked, finally feeling that we were on to something.

"Yeah, over there in Hermann Park. Bus go right by it." He gave us a bus number, which in our excitement we quickly forgot. There would be Juneteenth in Houston after all!

"Ya'll going to Galveston?" he inquired as he sat the plates of grits, sausage, and eggs in front of us. "They have somethin' goin' on down there too."

Wow! As it turned out, we *were* going to Galveston that morning to do some research on Juneteenth at the Rosenberg Library. The prospects of experiencing Juneteenth were improving.

"Yes, we're leaving right after breakfast," we answered. He gave us directions to Galveston, and called a young man from hotel management over to give us more details about Juneteenth events in Houston. We left him a hefty tip, for he had given us more than good service. He had renewed our hope.

The three days which followed this revelation were filled with activity. We made mental snapshots of all the images associated with Juneteenth. At last, Juneteenth was coming into focus and was taking center stage, competing admirably against the Rockets. From our mental and written notes, and our participation in Juneteenth, we quickly learned that it is not one experience or one event, but a wonderful blend of many things. However, it is foremost a freedom celebration.

Reading of the Emancipation Proclamation.

A Juneteenth picnic under a tent, Galveston, Texas.

JUNETEENTH began spontaneously on June 19, 1865, amidst shouts, dances, prayers, and songs as slaves in Galveston, Texas, reacted to the delayed news of freedom. Their impromptu celebrations spawned the folk festival known today as Juneteenth and, since 1866, descendants of former slaves have gathered yearly to celebrate it.

Juneteenth is an ethnic holiday which includes the reading of the Emancipation Proclamation and Proclamation #3, two documents which announced that slaves were free. Juneteenth is the retelling of the legends of how it got its name or why the news was late getting to Texas. It is a day or a week or a month of activities held in museums, parks, amphitheaters, and backyards. It is the small gatherings on Daufuskie Island, South Carolina, and the immense crowds in Buffalo, New York.

Enjoying the parade—Black cowboys and cowgirls march in Galveston, Texas.

Juneteenth is busloads, carloads, trainloads of Texans, who like migratory birds, are drawn back home on June nineteenth. It's class reunions and family reunions. Juneteenth includes parades: the clip-clop of horse hooves on cobblestone streets, and the rumble of army tanks as they wind their way around blocked-off streets. It is paper flowers on brightly decorated floats, and children pelting bystanders with generous handsful of candy. It is cowboys and cowgirls sitting high on prancing horses. It's sporting events such as baseball, footraces, and rodeos.

Juneteenth is children romping and playing in shady places. It is also mountains of food, and the smell of barbecue ribs cooking on open fires. It's the cool taste of chilled watermelon and creamy homemade ice cream. Juneteenth is music: the mellow sounds of blues and the upbeat tempo of gospel.

Finally, Juneteenth is the red, white, and blue of the American flag, and the brilliant bursts of fireworks. Juneteenth festivals crisscross the United States: Texas to Georgia, New York to California, Virginia to Arizona, and Louisiana to Washing-

Galveston Fire Department, Juneteenth, 1995.

ton, D.C. In a very real sense Juneteenth is the July Fourth equivalent for Black Americans—their freedom celebration which has become an expression of Black pride, solidarity, and cultural tradition.

What is the complete meaning of Juneteenth? How did it start? How did the Freedom Day celebration become known as Juneteenth? Why has it become such an important part of Black history? In the pages ahead we will explore these questions and look more fully at this expression of Black hope and pride.

Slaves honoring President Abraham Lincoln.

CHAPTER

2

FREE at last, free at last!" slaves shouted as they learned of their freedom. Depending on the region of the United States in which they lived, slaves received word of freedom at different times. The earliest announcement was made in Washington, D.C., on January 1, 1863, the date the Emancipation Proclamation went into effect. The latest official announcement was made in Galveston, Texas, on June 19, 1865, two months after the Civil War ended.

Slavery became an economic and political "hot potato" during the Civil War. Fiercely differing opinions in the North and the South about the abolition of slavery separated them from each other. When the two regions couldn't settle their differences, six Southern states, including Texas, seceded (pulled out) of the Union to form their own government. The new government was called the Confederate States of America.

In September, 1862, President Abraham Lincoln decided to use his authority as president and commander-in-chief of the Armed Forces to free slaves in the rebellious Confederate states. "Mr. Lincoln's Proclamation," hailed by America's former slaves as the document which freed them, did not free all of them. Freedom came to all Negro slaves, especially in the South and Southwest, as a result of Union control during the Civil War, the end the Civil War, and finally the ratification of the Thirteenth Amendment to the Constitution on December 6, 1865. The Thirteenth Amendment completely abolished slavery in the United States.

So, Texas slaves had good reason to rejoice on June 19, 1865. The Civil War had ended on April 9, the Union army had been sent to Texas to restore order and ensure that the Emancipation was enforced, and the Proclamation or General Order #3 was being read, informing them that they were free—free at last!

Official
HEADQUARTERS DISTRICT OF TEXAS
GALVESTON, TEXAS, June 19, 1865

General Order, #3

"The people are informed that in accordance with a proclamation from the Executive of the United States, all slaves are free. This involves an absolute equality of personal rights and rights of property, between former masters and slaves, and the connection heretofore existing between them, become that between employer and hired labor. The freed are advised to remain at their present homes, and work for wages. They are informed that they will not be allowed to collect at military posts; and that they will not be supported in idleness either there or elsewhere."

By order of
Major-General Granger,
F.W. Emery, Maj. & A.A.G.
(Signed,)

"All slaves are free." These few words, read at Ashton Villa in Galveston, Texas, caused an explosion of joy among the crowd of newly freed slaves! During the Union occupation of Galveston, Ashton Villa was headquarters for Major-General Granger and his staff. Streets and plantation lawns quickly brimmed with new Black citizens leaping, swaying, and whirling in unrehearsed glee.

"Soldiers all of a sudden wuz [was] everywha'. Comin' in bunches—crossin' and walkin' and ridin'. Everyone was singin'. We was all walking on golden clouds, hallelujah!" said former slave Felix Haywood.

The Proclamation or General Order #3, written and read by

Ashton Villa, Galveston, Texas, was once used as Headquarters for the Union. It is the site at which Proclamation #3 was read.

General Granger, was a shorter version of the Emancipation Proclamation. However, it included those all-important words, "all slaves are free," which slaves everywhere dreamed of one day hearing. Newly freed bondsmen related this day to the Jubilee in the Old Testament of the Bible when the Israelites were freed from bondage. Former slave Frank Adams of Texas said, "W'en freedom come, you hear bells, whistles, an' shoutin' eb'ry way [everywhere]."

A funny story about one woman's reaction to the news was told by former slave Anna Woods. She watched the curious behavior of the newly freed woman as she jumped on and off a barrel. The woman would jump on the barrel and she would shout. Then she would jump off the barrel and shout some more. It didn't matter to

Mount Sinai Youth Department Drill Team, 1990 Juneteenth Parade.

her that Anna Woods and others were looking at her strangely, for she kept up her weird ritual of jumping and shouting for a very long while.

During the days and months following June 19, 1865, slaves throughout Texas, Oklahoma, and Louisiana were called in from cotton fields, horse stables, and slave quarters to hear the Proclamation read. Over and over, former slaves were told either by their masters or Union soldiers that they were as free as they were. They were also told that they could leave the plantation or they could stay and work for shares of the crop. No matter who brought the news, slave reaction was the same. They were joyful, thankful, defiant, and, sometimes, a little suspicious.

There were many instances of slaves abruptly stopping whatever they were doing. Milk pails filled with warm milk were left in pastures. Hoes were dropped in cotton fields. Meals were unserved. Slaves scattered; some to find family members. Others left just because they were free to do it. In an interview, former slave Lucy Barnes related her experience. "I was standin' thar with my milk pail and I jest drap it [milk pail] on the groun' an' begin gettin' way," she said. Another ex-slave said that many freed men didn't know where they were going; they just went.

Joy was a natural reaction to freedom, but so was disbelief. Slaves couldn't believe that freedom had finally come. Some of them wanted to hear it repeated over and over again that they were free. Texas author Amelia Barr gave this account of how her former slave Harriet responded to the news of freedom. She said that she went into the kitchen to tell Harriet that she was free, and she saw her leaning against the open door looking toward the east. Harriet believed that freedom was going to come from the east. Her baby girl was on the floor playing with some empty thread spools. When

Fiddlers in the family.

Amelia Barr told Harriet that she was free, Harriet just looked at her. She was too stunned to speak. Finally, Harriet cried, "Say dem words again, Miss Milly! Say dem again."

Satisfied that her mistress was telling her the truth, Harriet darted over to her baby, threw her shoulder high and shrieked, "Tamar, you'se free! You'se free, Tamar!" Afterward, she checked her free baby's face, hands, and feet as though she had just given birth to her.

The news of freedom did not always come in the manner Harriet and other slaves thought it would. Many expected trumpets to sound and soldiers to ride in on white horses to free them, and they were very disappointed when this didn't happen.

"When dem Yankees coming, Miss Milly?" Harriet asked, still expecting some excitement to happen.

"Nobody knows," Amelia answered honestly.

"How I free then?" Harriet questioned.

"They sent word."

"Mighty poor way to set folks free," Harriet complained.

Freedom songs sprouted like dandelions, as free men and women put words and rhythm to freedom. "Free at Last, Free at Last. Thank God Almighty, I'm Free at Last" was one of the first freedom songs. Folk songs such as "Many Thousand Gone" were made up about work former slaves didn't have to do or the harsh treatment they no longer had to endure. "No more auction block for me. No more, no more. No more auction block for me, many thousand gone. No more hundred lash for me. No more, no more. No more hundred lash for me, many thousand gone," they sang joyously.

Former Virginia slave Charlotte Brown gave a vivid description of how freedom songs were created. She said that when the news came, the first reaction of newly liberated Blacks was to sing and shout. They shouted to songs which began with one person singing the lead, making up words and adding verses as he or she went along. Soon the musicians picked up the beat, and a new song was born. Shouting became more animated with the addition of each new verse. These musical celebrations lasted all day, and often began anew the next morning. "Chile, dat was one glorious time!" Mrs. Brown said.

News of freedom spread like the familiar Texas brushfire, traveling rapidly from one happy slave to another and from one Texas community to another. On the wharves of Galveston, Texas, joyful Black men pitched their hats high in the muggy June air, scattering the sea gulls which hovered nearby. Men and women screamed, "We's free! We's free."

But, not all slaves in the Southwest were told of their freedom on June 19, 1865. A few slaveholders continued to keep the news from them, hoping to harvest another cotton crop. Others told their slaves about the Proclamation, but dared them to leave the plantation. Texas slave narratives are filled with stories of hair-raising escapes to freedom after June 19. The escape of the mother of former slave Tempie Cummins reads like a chapter from a thriller novel.

"*She say she used to hide in the chimney corner and listen to what the white folks say. When freedom was 'clared, [declared] marster wouldn't tell 'em, but mother she hear him telln' mistus that the slaves was free but they didn' know it and he's not gwineter [going to] tell 'em till he makes another crop or two. When mother hear that she says she slip out of the chimney corner and clicked her heels together four times and shouts, 'I's free, I's free.' Then she runs to the field, 'gainst marster's will and tol' all the slaves and they quit*

All dressed up for Juneteenth, June 19, 1900.

work. Then she run away in the night. She slip into a big ravine near the house and have them bring me to her. Marster, he come out with his gun and shot at mother but she run down the ravine and gits away with me."

Texas-style tall tales and legends which explain why the news of emancipation reached Texas two years, six months, and eighteen days late have been passed down from generation to generation. One legend tells of how a messenger was sent with the Proclamation, but was ambushed and killed before reaching Texas. Another legend has President Lincoln attempting to deliver the news himself. He didn't make it either. Yet another story claims that the news of freedom came by boat to Galveston, Texas, on June 17. According to this legend, Black stevedores who were loading and unloading ships at Pier 21 got wind of the news, and leaked it before the official announcement was made. A favorite legend among Black Texans, though, is the one about the Negro messenger who was personally sent by President Lincoln to deliver the Emancipation Proclamation to Texas. He left Washington, D.C., on January 1, 1863, riding a very slow and ornery mule. The mule was so slow and contrary, and the courier made so many stops that it took him two and a half years to get to Texas. He finally arrived in Texas or Oklahoma (depending upon who is telling the story) on June 19, 1865.

The story which is probably closest to the truth is the one which shows the unwillingness of Texas slave owners to free their slaves before their cotton crops were gathered. Wendy Watriss, a Texas photo-journalist, recorded an elderly Texas woman's version of the legend of the late news.

"I'll tell you like they told me. The 19th is the day the white people gave those Negroes for their celebration. When they freed the

Negro, when the war was over, all these farmers had crops and slaves and they had all their money tied up in them. If they had cut the slaves off right away, they would have been broke men. So they didn't say anything. Made them work until the 19th of June when all the crops were cleaned and all the work was over with. Then they gave them that day for their celebration."

Remembering Dr. Martin Luther King, Jr., in a Juneteenth parade.

CHAPTER

3

—

FROM the very beginning, Juneteenth was part revival and part family reunion and homecoming. It has always been a special time for Black families to get together to have fun and to celebrate their past history. Black Texans named these gatherings "June 19," "Jamboree," "Freedom Day," and "Emancipation Day." However, Juneteenth is the name which has stuck. Some folks say that Juneteenth got its name from a little girl who was much too excited to take the time to clearly pronounce June *and* nineteenth. Others say that the little girl had a speech defect and couldn't say June nineteenth.

"It's June teenth," she responded when someone asked her what the day was. But, most people agree that the name Juneteenth probably came about from blending the month and day in which Black Texans were set free (June and nineteenth).

The first recorded Juneteenth celebrations were held in Texas in 1866, one year after the slaves were liberated. These earliest Juneteenth festivals set the pattern for the ones which followed. They were colorful, festive events very much like the Fourth of July celebrations which in the past former slaves had attended with their masters. A mid-morning parade, a commemoration ceremony, worship service, picnics, ball games, and dances were just some of the activities packed into the long Emancipation Day celebrations.

The parades, which usually began around ten o'clock in the morning, started Juneteenth on a festive note. In the early days, Juneteenth parades were led by Negro brass bands which had a reputation for playing "soul-stirring" music. Some of these bands came from as far away as Louisiana to perform. Next in the parade lineup were former slaves, including those who had run away to

Musicians performing at East Woods Park, June 19, 1900, Austin, Texas.

become soldiers in the Union army. In a few localities former slaves held separate celebrations because they believed that the "young folks" (Blacks born after slavery) did not have the same appreciation of Emancipation Day as they did.

Blacks who belonged to lodges and self-help groups made up a very large portion of the parade. They dressed in their finest lodge uniforms decorated with brightly colored sashes, rosettes, and stars. These high-stepping, colorfully dressed men and women were a real hit with parade watchers.

Grandstand, June 19, 1900, East Woods Park.

By 1900, the parade also included the more well-to-do Blacks who rode beautiful horses and buggies covered with ribbons, flowers, and streamers. But, Blacks who were not so fortunate were in the parade, too. They rented their horses and buggies from the local livery stables for the day. Weather-beaten farm wagons were changed into lively historical floats to represent the slaves' flight to freedom. Lighted torches, held high by triumphant marchers, symbolized the hard-earned freedom of the Negro, and axes were carried to signify the cutting of slavery chains.

While Juneteenth was filled with special moments, none was more important than the reading of the Emancipation Proclamation. It was read with great flair and drama by the most highly regarded person in the community. The annual reading of the Proclamation reminded Blacks of their freedom and their citizenship in America. Next, Juneteenth speeches were delivered by former slaves, military men, religious leaders, and educators. Their speeches were usually very patriotic, and called attention to the importance of remembering their struggle to be free.

The June 10, 1876, issue of *The Waco Examiner* reported a Major Alford as saying, *"Friends and fellow citizens, the proclamation of emancipation that sounded through the land thirteen years ago today, and that great event which made us free men has made the 19th of June the dearest day of the three hundred and sixty-five to us. It is our Fourth of July."*

At the end of his speech, he appealed to his listeners to work hard and to always practice honesty. He wanted them to avoid being accused of laziness or of lacking ambition. He knew very well that the recently passed vagrancy laws were aimed at Black men, many of whom were already in jail for the crime of loitering.

"...it [freedom] means industry and honesty, and it is only those

Watermelon wagon, Austin, Texas.

of us who are industrious and honest that are free," Major Alford warned.

Everyone was encouraged to participate in the spirited songs of freedom and patriotism at Juneteenth. Negro spirituals such as "In the Great Getting Up Morning" and "Free at Last" were two of their favorite songs because they expressed the joy of being free. On the other hand, "The Star-Spangled Banner" and "America the Beautiful" were sung to show pride in their newly won American citizenship.

Seniors view the parade from their comfortable bench.

CHAPTER

4

———

TEN short years after the news arrived in Texas, Juneteenth or Emancipation Day had already become a respected freedom celebration, enjoyed by Blacks and whites alike. The June 19, 1875, issue of *The Galveston Daily News* reported, "No doubt the colored men will rejoice in contemplating that instrument signed by Abraham Lincoln, whereby was given unto him his freedom." Other newspapers commented on the orderliness of Juneteenth gatherings, and were amazed at the number of people who attended. In the bigger cities and towns, crowds numbered in the thousands. *The Waco Examiner* reported that more than two thousand Blacks gathered for the 1876 Emancipation Day parade under the threat of a downpour of rain. "...notwithstanding the heavy black clouds that every moment threatened to deluge the earth with water, the procession formed at 10:00 o'clock."

Different communities celebrated Juneteenth in different ways. Larger cities and towns held elaborate parades and ceremonies while rural communities celebrated mainly with family picnics and ball games.

Worship service was an important part of many celebrations.

Sometimes services were held in local churches. At other times, they were held in public parks. Although ministers didn't always agree that the park was the proper place for worship, they still delivered revival-like freedom sermons. Not all communities observed Juneteenth with religious services, though. For them, Juneteenth was just another day to have fun, and that was the way they wanted to keep it.

The high points of the day for children were the afternoon picnics. They could eat as much as they liked, and they were free to rollick in the wide open space of the park. Youngsters also enjoyed competing against each other in softball games, horseshoe pitching, sack racing, foot racing, and rope pulling. The cakewalk dance was another popular activity which appealed to children and adults. This competitive dance, which began on the plantations, was first known as the chalkwalk. It later became a couples dance. The cakewalk was performed to see which dancers could outdo the other with the highest kicks, the fastest steps, and the most daring leaps and turns, all while balancing a pail of water on their heads. The couple who spilled the least amount of water won the prize. By the time the dance was introduced into the activities at Juneteenth, the prize was a cake. Thus, its name—cakewalk.

Laughter and shrieks filled the parks as children chased and romped.

"We would have games, barrel-rolling and the men would play baseball and go fishing. Everything was free and it would be from sunup to well into the night," Juneteenth organizer LaVerne Ross told a reporter from the *Santa Monica Outlook*.

Picnics began in the early afternoon and lasted until dark. Barbecue chicken, beef and pork, potato salad, watermelons, and heaps of delicious desserts were spread out on long plank tables for everyone to share. Children took turns fanning the flies which were attracted to the delicious food. Women made homemade ice cream in crank ice-cream freezers, and they sold pies and cakes to raise money for scholarships. They also made a special brand of red soda pop which was heartily consumed by thirsty youngsters. The red pop was a mixture of food coloring, lemons, sugar, and water. It probably tasted like our pink lemonade of today. Juneteenth was the only day of the year when children could drink as much of this mixture as they wanted. Everybody was welcome to share in the bountiful supply of food and drinks. After all, it was a community celebration.

LaVerne Ross remembered how excited she was as a child when Juneteenth neared. For the first fifteen years of her life, she and her family got up before daybreak to travel approximately 128 miles from Malone, Texas, to Comanche Crossing to observe Juneteenth. Comanche Crossing was one of the first sites of Juneteenth.

"All of the mothers would have their own crafts or they would have barbecue all over the place and watermelon, watermelon," said Ms. Ross.

Former Texan Willie Barner, who now lives in Los Angeles, California, said that Juneteenth meant more to him than Christmas. On Juneteenth, he would be assured of

A young majorette poised and ready to march in Galveston, Texas.

getting a new outfit to wear, and of spending the whole day having fun.

Juneteenth was and still is best known for its barbecue. Texan Lawrence Crouchett recalled what Juneteenth was like for him in the early 1930s. He said that the excitement would start two to three days before June 19. That was when the men killed the cattle and dug eighteen-foot trenches for the barbecue. Then they would sit around in the park all night on June 18 to cook and "hurrah." During their all-night vigil, they told stories and teased each other about losing the upcoming baseball games or races. Women stayed up all night, too. They made pies, cakes, and potato salad enough to feed an army of people. They were anticipating that family and friends would be coming from near and far to share in the eating and fun.

CHAPTER
5
___

IN the early 1900s, Black Texans left the state in large numbers. They were trying to escape the hard life as sharecroppers. Share-croppers were people who lived on someone else's farm and worked the farm for a share of the crop.

By the end of the year, they had used up their "share" in food, shelter, seeds, and other necessities. Most often, tenants ended up owing the landlords money. Therefore, they never had enough money to buy property or to better their living conditions. Share-cropping promoted a cycle of poverty which would always keep them down and indebted to the owner of the farm.

Added to the burden of poverty was the fear of lynchings and other acts of terror by white supremacist groups like the Ku Klux Klan. So, Black Texans migrated by the thousands to "The Promised Land"—places of safety, jobs, and education. A large number of Black Texans migrated to Kansas, Arkansas, Oklahoma, Missouri, and California in search of a better life.

Whenever people move from one home or one town to another, they take more than their personal belongings with them. They take their memories, too. They take with them memories of special people and celebrations, and those memories keep them connected to their past. Thus, wherever they settled, Black Texans remembered Juneteenth. They remembered the family reunions, the colorful parades, the freedom speeches, and the wonderful picnics. How could they forget the smell of barbecue cooking all night or cranking ice-cream churns until their arms were sore? How could they forget the baseball games or the "tie downs" [calf ropings] and rodeos?

Slowly, they began to organize Juneteenth celebrations in their new hometowns. Of course, if it was possible for them to return

Moving West. Blacks migrated west in search of a better life. Many found employment with the railroad.

home to Texas, they did. For those who could not, the next best thing was to have their *own* Juneteenth celebrations in the style of the ones they remembered. So, the spread of Juneteenth began. Many Juneteenth observances began as family reunions. Others began as separate state celebrations within the same community. People from Oklahoma would gather in one park while people from Arkansas would gather in another. But, they were gathering for the same reason: to celebrate emancipation. These gatherings soon grew and combined into much larger events.

Representative Al Edwards with his family at Juneteenth, 1979.

During the 1970s, race pride became one of the most important issues in the Black community. More and more Juneteenth celebrations were held to highlight the accomplishments of Blacks in America. Representative Al Edwards of Houston, Texas, used the growing interest in Black pride to introduce a bill in the Texas legislature to make June 19 a legal holiday in Texas. The bill was approved by the legislature on June 7, 1979, and became a legal holiday on January 1, 1980. It is the first and still the only official holiday for an emancipation celebration in the United States.

In 1979, huge Juneteenth events were held to celebrate the passing of the bill. That year, Austin, Texas, had one of the largest Juneteenth celebrations in its history. It was a five-day party which included a tennis tournament, music, poetry recitals, plays, dances, a carnival, and many sports activities.

That same year, neighboring Columbus, Texas, held a more traditional Juneteenth at County Camp on the Colorado River. Cakewalk dance competitions, turkey shoots, fishing, swimming, and hayrides brought back memories of earlier Juneteenths.

Convention of Freedmen discussing their political rights.

CHAPTER
6
—

JUNETEENTH has grown from a mere whisper during World Wars I and II, when celebrations were suspended, to a loud shout in the 1990s, as its popularity soars. During this seventy-year span, Juneteenth has survived the embarrassment of Texans about the news arriving so late. It has withstood criticism from some Blacks that it glorifies bondage rather than freedom, and it has overcome the apathy of Blacks during the fifties and sixties.

More and more, June 19 has become the day on which Juneteenth celebrations are brought to a close. Leading up to this special day, there are many fun-filled and educational events which range from concerts featuring famous entertainers, to pageants and Black history tours. Working together with the local newspapers, radio and television stations, Juneteenth organizers ensure that the news about Juneteenth reaches the community.

Juneteenth is for everyone! People of different social, religious, and ethnic backgrounds get caught up in the spirit of Juneteenth, and they work together to plan events for everyone to enjoy. One of the best examples of this kind of cooperation was seen in Galveston, Texas. In 1995, the Texas Seaport Museum, the Galveston

Mrs. Lois Holden, niece Brenda Womack, and great-nephew join in protesting unfair journalism.

"We Are Sisters" sisterhood float in parade.

Historical Society, and the Galveston Branch of the NAACP came together to sponsor three weeks of Juneteenth activities.

On June 19, 1995, combined church choirs sang Negro spirituals and patriotic songs while the audience swayed and clapped to the beat. Local Black leaders and preachers made speeches about the importance of remembering how freedom came to Texas. It was also a time of protest. Blacks were protesting the unfair reporting practices of one of the local newspapers. They encouraged people to carry signs and wear T-shirts which read, "Unfair Journalism!!"

Also, parents of school-aged children coaxed their reluctant children out of bed to share in the early morning continental breakfast at Ashton Villa and to listen to the reading of Proclamation #3. Moms and dads made sure that their children understood that Juneteenth is more than a holiday from school. It is a celebration of freedom.

At the same time, forty miles away, Hermann Park in Houston, Texas, was filling up as picnickers and spectators staked out their places on the grassy knoll in front of Miller Outdoor Theater. By midday, "Hippy Knoll," named for the flower children who gathered there in the sixties, was peppered with blankets, lawn chairs, baby strollers, and droves of people waiting for the Juneteenth program and entertainment to begin.

"Hippie Knoll," Herman Park, Houston, Texas.

The line forms for barbecue and watermelon at Miller Outdoor Theater.

Families found shady spaces under sprawling trees, but stayed within earshot of the theater. They unloaded steamers and barbecue grills from vans and the beds of pickup trucks, and quickly loaded them with link sausages, barbecue ribs, and hot dogs. The aroma of spicy barbecue and charcoal mingled in the steamy June air, filling the park and enticing hungry folks to join in the feast.

Umbrellas popped up like mushrooms on a neglected lawn as those who were not lucky enough to find a shade tree tried to hide from the sweltering sun. The theme for this year's Juneteenth was "Teachers: Builders of Our Heritage—Key to America's Future." Houston's reigning Miss Juneteenth, Erika Freeman, read the Emancipation Proclamation, and other members of her court gave speeches. Several teachers were honored for their dedicated service to children.

Soon, hundreds of senior citizens filled the huge stage to receive words of gratitude and praise from the speakers. Here again, Houstonians were keeping tradition. They were honoring their elders. Jazz, blues, and rock bands took the stage, playing the latest tunes and inviting people to clap their hands and sing along if they wished. Those people who didn't have picnic lunches or barbecue grills formed a long, winding line around Miller Theater

(From left) Janine Bell, President of Elegba Folklore Society, greets the assembly at Juneteenth, 1995, in Richmond, Virginia.

Civil Rights attorney, Oliver W. Hill, is an elder. He was honored for his work in the Civil Rights movement.

Making beautiful music — Elegba Folklore Society.

Carl Jackson does "Angeline Johnson."

and waited patiently to get a taste of the famous Texas barbecue and a cold slice of sweet watermelon. The finale was the spectacular fireworks display which lit up the warm night sky, bringing a sparkling end to another emancipation day—Juneteenth.

Like the sparks from the traditional fireworks displays which end many Juneteenth observances, new freedom celebrations are being ignited. Juneteenth festivals are presently held in every region of the United States.

The 1987 Juneteenth celebration in Atlanta, Georgia, was held on a ranch owned by James Holt, and it included everything from hayrides to quarter-horse racing. The festival began at 1:00 P.M. and lasted until "the cows came home," he said. Even the small island of Daufuskie, South Carolina, salutes June 19 annually with crab feasts and oyster roasts. Buffalo, New York, has one of the largest celebrations outside of Texas, boasting up to fifteen thousand people in attendance.

Each year since 1988, Anacostia Museum in Washington, D.C., is changed into a carnival-like setting with booths and stages for dancing, speeches, storytelling, games, and other fun activities. Anacostia is just one of many museums which have taken the lead in organizing and sponsoring Juneteenth festivals.

In 1991, Santa Monica, California, held its first "40 Acres and a Mule Juneteenth Family Picnic." Sponsored by the NAACP, the free event featured live music, horseshoe throwing, basketball, barbecued ribs, and chicken. In cities like Oakland, California, and

Minneapolis, Minnesota, attendance at Juneteenth has grown from one thousand to fifteen thousand.

Blacks in Tucson, Arizona, have been celebrating Juneteenth for over twenty-five years. According to Raina Wagner of the *Arizona Daily Star*, the first Juneteenth celebrations consisted of a few Black families gathered for a picnic. Over the years, the family picnics in Tucson have grown into major annual Juneteenth events which bring families and friends and all races together.

"Juneteenth is important to everyone, it doesn't matter what color your skin is," said Juanita Stewart, who, with her husband, Bill, are Juneteenth organizers in Tucson.

Richmond, Virginia, held its first Juneteenth Emancipation Day Heritage Celebration at the Virginia Historical Society the afternoon of June 16, 1996. Patterned after the Texas Juneteenth festivals, Richmond's celebration included a processional of the elders (older people, local leaders, and politicians) who were escorted in by drummers, African dancers, and a jazz bagpiper. It also included the familiar reading of the Proclamation #3 by Janine Bell, president of *Elegba Folklore Society*, and the recognition of local and state politicians. Richmond's most highly respected civil rights lawyer, Mr. Oliver W. Hill, was honored for his contributions to ensuring the freedom of Black citizens in Virginia and in the country.

Claiming a space at Hermann Park in Houston.

Drummers and dancers escort the elders in.

Co-sponsored by the *Eleg*ba Folklore Society and the Virginia Historical Society, the Juneteenth Emancipation Day Heritage Celebration also featured a jazz rendition of "Amazing Grace" by the nation's only Black jazz bagpipe player, Rufus Harley, of Philadelphia, Pennsylvania, a reenactment of the 54th Massachusetts Regiment by local Civil War reenactors, energetic African dances performed by the *Eleg*ba folklore dancers, lectures on Reconstruction by local historians and professors, a dramatization

(From left) Getting ready. Rufus Harley, world's only jazz bagpipe player.
"At ease." Dr. Kenneth Brown, Massachusetts 54th Colored Regiment reenactor.

by Carl Jackson of Paul Lawrence Dunbar's "When My Lias Went to War," a poem about a Black boy who served in the Civil War, and another poem, "Angelina Johnson," about the most beautiful and eligible Black woman in town. Excerpts from Reverend John Jaspers' celebrated sermon "De Sun Do Move" were recited by Reverend John Johnson, and children had fun making music with Dr. S.O. Feelgood of the Dr. S.O. Feelgood Band & Show.

MY initial fear that I would not experience Juneteenth has been allayed. I discovered over the last two years that Juneteenth is not one event, but a series of events which celebrate the most basic of all human rights: freedom. I cannot recall the precise moment or moments when I felt the spirit of Juneteenth. Maybe it was an accumulation of experiences. Perhaps it was the anticipation as Willis and I drove the forty miles from Houston to Galveston after we were told that Juneteenth events were being held there. Maybe it was seeing the sun add hues of pink to the blue of the early morning sky, foretelling a beautiful day ahead. Or it could have happened when I walked out on Pier 21 in Galveston, Texas, and gazed out over the glistening waters of the Galveston River, trying to imagine what it must have been like on the wharf when freedom was announced over 130 years ago.

Perhaps I understood better as I watched a warm exchange between a father and his toddler as they waited for Juneteenth to begin. He was quietly reading over the program in his lap, and she was craning her neck to see it. Moments later, she reached for the program. With the pacifier bobbing up and down in her mouth, the toddler listened with the interest of an adult as her dad explained what would be happening on this Juneteenth Day.

Maybe it happened as I sat on the cool grass beside young Alfred Williams, who was sitting in the shade of his grandfather's shadow. With earphones hanging around his neck and a Walkman in his lap, Alfred was obviously planning to tune Juneteenth out. But, like the rest of us, he was unable to resist listening to the gospel songs sung by soloist Melba Williams. He was intrigued by Representative Al Edwards's story of how he pushed his Juneteenth bill through the Texas legislature. Representative Edwards said that

Father and daughter enjoy a special moment at Juneteenth, Galveston, 1995.

Juneteenth gathering.

a number of legislators had agreed to support the bill, but several of them were still holding out. One representative told Mr. Edwards that he just couldn't support his Juneteenth bill because he didn't have any colored folks in his district. However, this same individual wanted to get a particular farm bill passed. "And, I told him, well, I don't have any farms in my district. So let's compromise," he chuckled.

I certainly know that I felt a great surge of pride on June 16, 1996, as I sat beneath an umbrella in front of the Virginia Historical Society in Richmond, Virginia. Waiting for the Juneteenth event to begin, I had time to reflect on how far Virginia had come. Today, two groups who heretofore seemed to have little in common were co-sponsoring Juneteenth and recognizing it as a legitimate Black folk festival.

Finally, the picture of Juneteenth was in focus. It was clear. Juneteenth is a gigantic collage of history, legends, family, speeches, parades, sports events, thanksgiving, and remembrance that is being posted for Americans everywhere to see and enjoy.

Williams family at Ashton Villa.

Organize Your Own Juneteenth

YOUR Juneteenth celebration can be as small as a family picnic in the park or as large as a community event. Juneteenth is a family affair. Therefore, you should ask your parents or other adult family members to help you organize the celebration.

Begin planning early enough to include neighbors, local city council or town council people, churches, mosques and synagogues, schools and colleges, and community organizations such as Scouts. Write a letter to these organizations stating your purpose and asking them to participate.

Next, plan the activities or events you would like to include in the celebration. You may want to sponsor a softball or baseball game. Or, you may want to have a skating party as a part of your celebration. Whatever you plan, make sure you include time in your program to read the Emancipation Proclamation or Proclamation #3. That is a very important tradition in any Juneteenth celebration.

Finally, call or write the local newspapers, radio or television stations to have them announce your Juneteenth event.

If you plan a family get-together, you will still need to plan ahead. Invite family from out of town to join you at a local park or in your backyard. Tell them, also, why Juneteenth is important and why your family should remember it. Ask one of the older members of the family to read the Emancipation Proclamation before the picnic begins.

Several national organizations may give you information on how you can plan a Juneteenth celebration.

National Emancipation Association, Inc.
2314 Wheeler
Houston, Texas 77004

Juneteenth, USA
c/o Representative Al Edwards
4913 1/2 Griggs
Houston, Texas 77021

Bibliography

BOOKS

Armstead, Bert Carson, Jr. *Galveston During the Civil War, 1861-65*, Masters Thesis. Texas Southern University, 1974.

Barr, Alwyn. *Black Texans: A History of Negroes in Texas, 1528-1971.* Austin: Jenkins Publishing Company, 1973.

Barr, Amelia. *All the Days of My Life.* New York: D. Appleton, 1913, (1923) 2nd printing.

Cohen, Henning, et al. *The Folklore of American Holidays.* Detroit: Gale Research Associates, 1987.

Fehrenbach, T.R. *Lone Star: A History of Texas and Texans.* New York: Macmillan Publishing Company, Inc., 1977.

Franklin, John Hope. *The Emancipation Proclamation.* Garden City, New York: Doubleday & Company, 1963.

Grey, Amy. *Juneteenth, A Historical Perspective: A Research Paper.* Washington, D.C. Anacostia Museum, Smithsonian Institution, 1991.

Pemberton, Doris Hollis. *Juneteenth at Comanche Crossing.* Austin: Eakin Press, 1983.

Perdue, Charles, et. al. *Weevils in the Wheat: Interviews with Virginia Slaves.* Charlottesville, Virginia: University Press, 1976.

Rawick, George P., General Editor. *The American Slave: A Composite Autobiography, Supplement/Series 2, Volume 2, Texas Slave Narratives, pts. 1–2.* (WPA), 1972.

Rawick, George P., et. al. *The American Slave: A Composite Autobiogra-*

phy, Texas Narratives, Parts 1, 2, 3, and 5. Westport, Connecticut: Greenwood Press, Inc., 1979.

Rawick, George P., et. al. *The American Slave: A Composite Autobiography, Arkansas Slave Narrative*, Vol. 11, Part 7, 1979.

Rice, Lawrence D. *The Negro in Texas, 1874-1900*. Baton Rouge, Louisiana: Louisiana State University Press, 1971.

Sance, Melvin M. *The Afro-American Texans*. San Antonio: University of Texas Institute of Texan Cultures at San Antonio, 1987

Shorto, Russell. *Abraham Lincoln and the End of Slavery*. Brookfield, CT: Millbrook Press, 1991.

Simond, Ada. *Let's Pretend: Mae Dee and Her Family Join Juneteenth Celebration*. Austin: Stevenson Press, 1978.

Smallwood, James M. *Time of Hope, Time of Despair*. New York: Kennikat Press, 1980.

Stoeltje, Beverly J. "Festivals in America," *Handbook of American Folklore*. Richard M. Dorson, editor. Bloomington, IN: University Press, 1983.

Tyler, Ronnie & Lawrence R. Murphy. *The Slave Narratives of Texas*. Austin: Encino Press, 1974.

Wiggins, William H., Jr. *Oh, Freedom!: Afro-American Emancipation Celebrations*. Knoxville, TN: University of Tennessee Press, 1987.

Williams, Davis A. *Juneteenth: Unique Heritage*. Austin: Texas African-American Heritage, Inc., 1992.

PERIODICALS

Bennett, Lerone, Jr., "Jubilee," *Ebony*, February, 1972, pp. 37-46. "Juneteenth: Texas Carries on Tradition of Emancipation Holiday with Amusement Park Celebration," *Ebony*, June, 1951, p. 30.

Prather, Patricia Smith. "A Celebration of Freedom," *Texas Highways*, June, 1988, pp. 2-8.

Ramsdell, Charles. "Texas from the Fall of the Confederacy to the Beginning of Reconstruction," Quarterly of Texas State Historical Association, XI (January, 1908), p. 204.

Rosson, Chester. "Juneteenth," *Texas Monthly*, June, 1988, p. 110.

Watriss, Wendy. "Celebrate Freedom," *Southern Exposure*, Vol. 5 (1), 1997, pp. 80-87.

Wiggins, William H., Jr., "Juneteenth," *American Visions*, June/July, 1993, pp. 30-31.

———"Juneteenth: They Closed the Town Up, Man!"
American Visions, June/July, 1986, pp. 40-45.

NEWSPAPERS

The Arizona Daily Star, June 13, 1996, Section D, p. 1.

Atlanta Now (special edition), 1991, p. 14

"The Celebration Yesterday," *Galveston Daily News*, June 20, 1875.

"Emancipation Day," *Galveston Daily News*, June 20, 1878.

Galveston Daily News, June 21, 1865, p. 1

Galveston Weekly News, June 28, 1865.

"Juneteenth Celebrates Slave Freedom in Texas," Austin, TX, *Sunday Express-News*, June 15, 1986, pp. 12–13.

"Juneteenth in Texas: Reinvigorating a Celebration," *The Washington Post*, June 20, 1990.

"Juneteenth Is Celebrated in California," *Houston Chronicle*, June 19, 1991, 1D, 10D.

"40 Acres & A Mule Juneteenth Family Picnic," *Santa Monica Outlook*, June 16, 1993, A4.

"Procession Yesterday," *Galveston Daily News*, June 21, 1870, p. 3.

"Think, Then Act: Why Did Lincoln Wait Until 1863..." by Joel Achenbach, *Washington Post*, July 21, 1995, p. C5.

Index